WORLD FAMOUS BUILDINGS

Sydney Opera House

by Alicia Z. Klepeis

BLASTOFF! READERS 3

BELLWETHER MEDIA • MINNEAPOLIS, MN

Blastoff! Readers are carefully developed by literacy experts to build reading stamina and move students toward fluency by combining standards-based content with developmentally appropriate text.

Level 1 provides the most support through repetition of high-frequency words, light text, predictable sentence patterns, and strong visual support.

Level 2 offers early readers a bit more challenge through varied sentences, increased text load, and text-supportive special features.

Level 3 advances early-fluent readers toward fluency through increased text load, less reliance on photos, advancing concepts, longer sentences, and more complex special features.

★ **Blastoff! Universe**

Reading Level

Blastoff! Beginners — Grade K

Blastoff! Readers — Grades 1–3

Blastoff! Discovery — Grade 4

This edition first published in 2026 by Bellwether Media, Inc.

Library of Congress Cataloging-in-Publication Data

LC record for Sydney Opera House available at: https://lccn.loc.gov/2025021803

Editor: Megan Borgert-Spaniol Series Designer: Chase Demmin

Printed in the United States of America, North Mankato, MN.

Table of Contents

What Is the Sydney Opera House?

The Sydney **Opera** House is a famous building. It is in Sydney, Australia. It sits on the edge of the city's harbor.

The opera house stands out. Its roof is made up of several large shells!

The Sydney Opera House is a center for performing arts. Visitors go there to see concerts and plays.

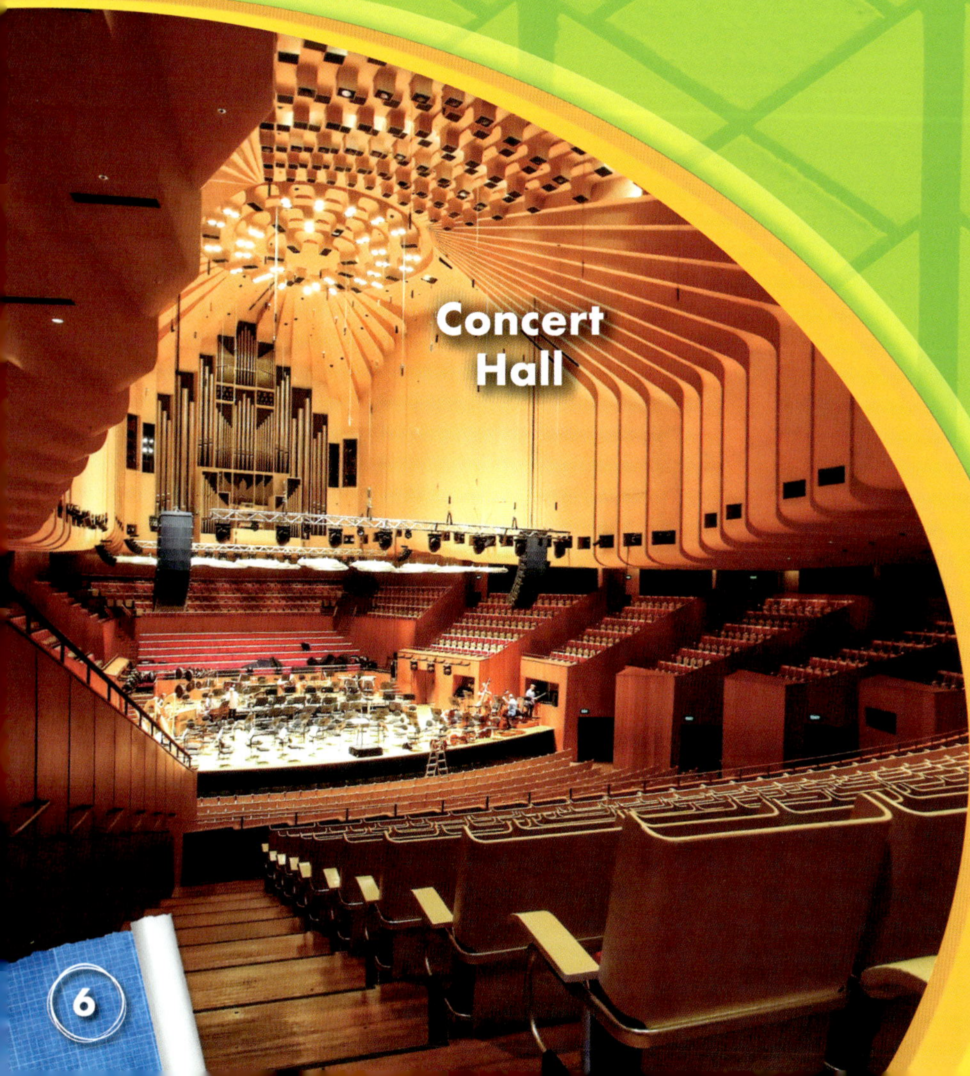

They can also visit several restaurants.

History of the Sydney Opera House

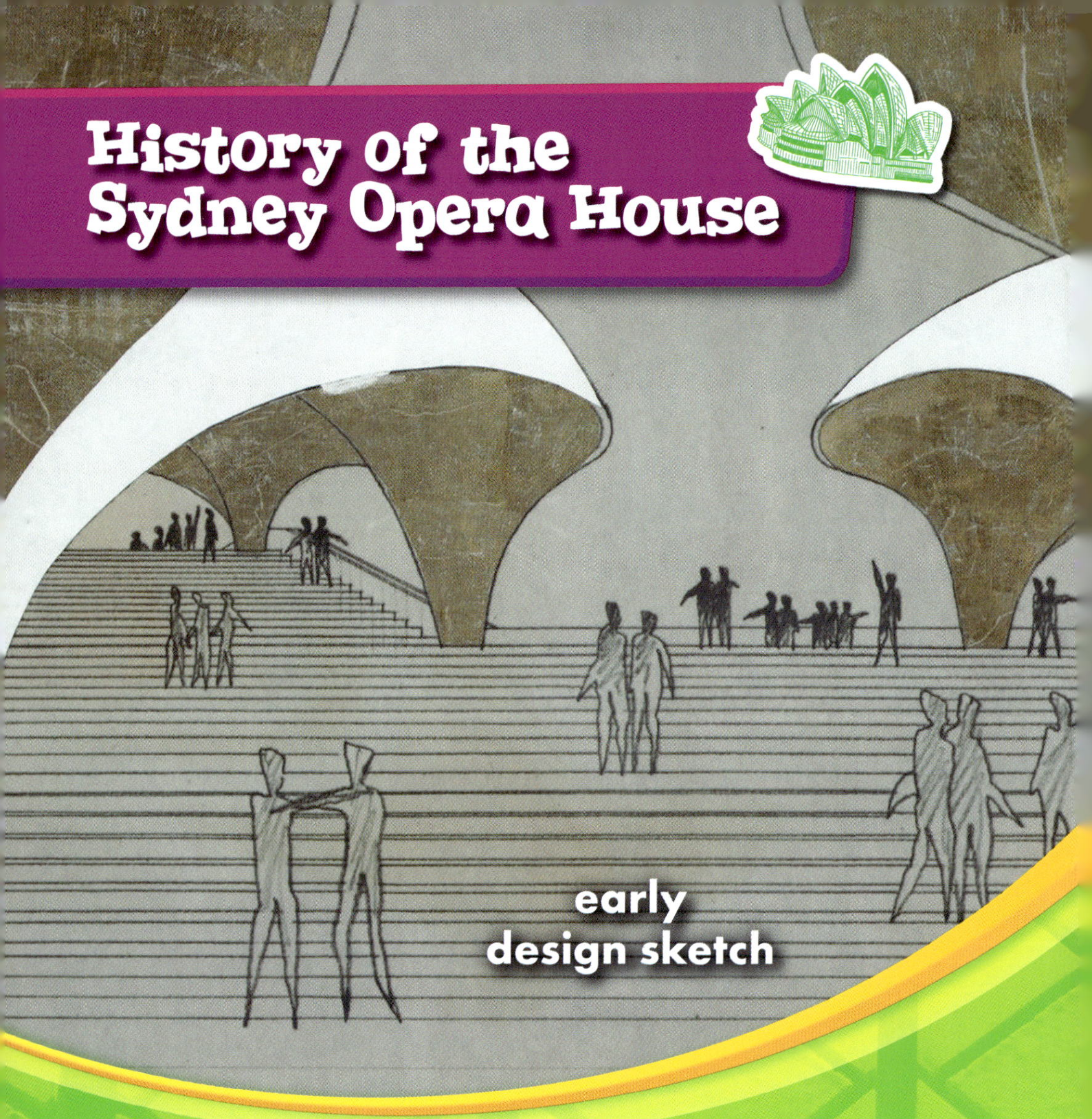

early design sketch

In the 1950s, leaders wanted Sydney to be a center for the arts.

They held a contest to **design** a national opera house. Danish **architect** Jørn Utzon won.

Jørn Utzon

Building began in 1959. Workers pushed **piles** made of steel and **concrete** into the ground. They poured concrete between the piles. This formed the building's **foundation**.

Then, workers built a concrete **podium** on top.

podium

Workers used **molds** to form concrete roof tiles. They connected the tiles to make the roof's shells.

Building Supplies

Workers finished the building's **interior** last. They built a concert hall and theaters for operas, plays, and more. The building opened in 1973.

Parts of the Sydney Opera House

The roof of the Sydney Opera House stands out. Some people think the roof's shells look like sailboat sails.

The roof's smooth tiles make the building shine in daylight. The smooth tiles also keep dirt away.

Terrific Tiles

Number of Tiles Used	more than 1 million
Number of Shells	10

The Sydney Opera House has several spaces for events. The largest is the Concert Hall. Its **organ** has over 10,000 pipes!

Size Comparison

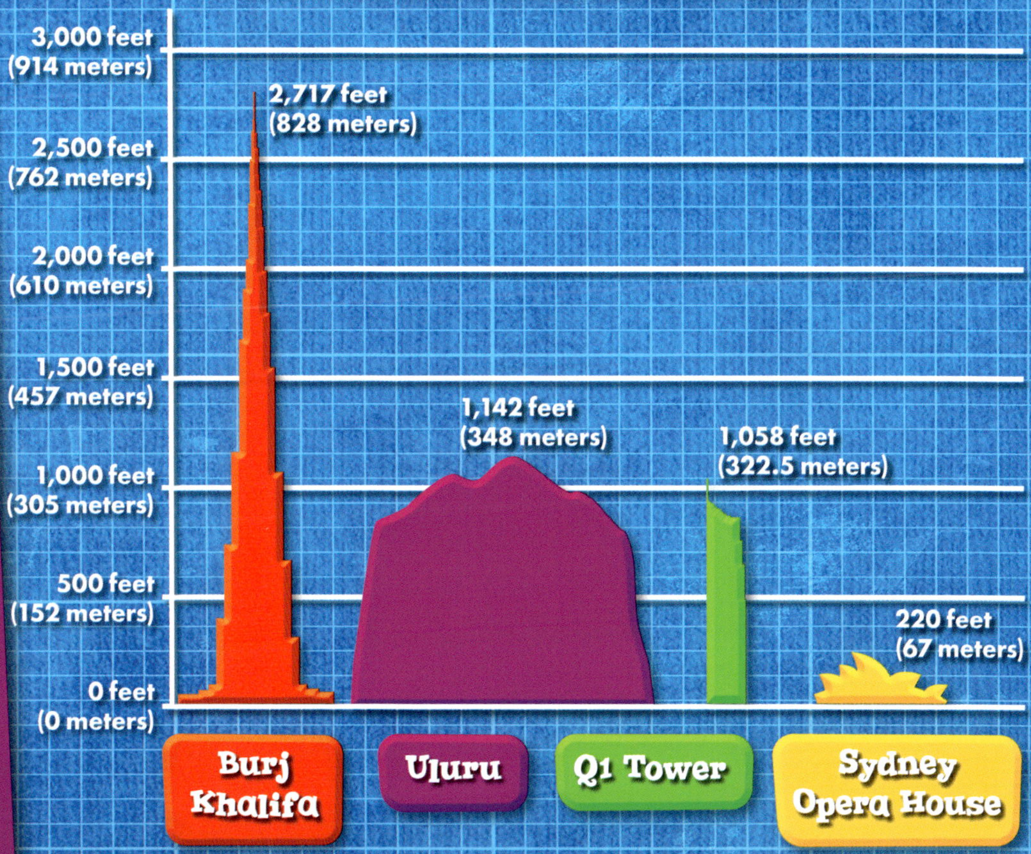

The building also has areas to gather and eat. Glass walls let in light and offer views of the harbor.

The Sydney Opera House Today

Nearly 11 million visitors go to the Sydney Opera House each year. It is one of Australia's most popular places.

Workers improved the building's **acoustics** in recent years. They also made the building more **accessible** for people in wheelchairs.

The Sydney Opera House hosts many events each year. These events include concerts, dances, plays, and more.

The opera house truly is a center for the arts!

QUAY WEST
AON
SHANGRI

Glossary

accessible—able to be used by people of all abilities

acoustics—the qualities of an enclosed space that make it easy or hard for a person in it to hear sounds

architect—a person who designs and plans buildings

concrete—a hard, strong building material made with cement, sand, rocks, and water

design—to make a plan for a building, object, or pattern

foundation—the base or support on which a building rests

interior—the inside of a building

molds—open containers in which substances can be shaped

opera—relating to a play in which the actors sing instead of speak

organ—a musical instrument made up of keyboards and pipes

piles—heavy beams or posts driven into the ground to support the foundation of a building

podium—a raised platform

To Learn More

AT THE LIBRARY

Colson, Rob. *The Spectacular Science of Buildings: From Ancient Wonders to Modern Megastructures.* London, U.K.: Kingfisher, 2023.

Neely, Jenna. *Would You Rather...Sing at Stonehenge or the Sydney Opera House?...and Other Well-Traveled Questions About the World's Wonders.* Chicago, Ill.: World Book, 2023.

Sabelko, Rebecca. *Australia.* Minneapolis, Minn.: Bellwether Media, 2023.

ON THE WEB

FACTSURFER

Factsurfer.com gives you a safe, fun way to find more information.

1. Go to www.factsurfer.com.
2. Enter "Sydney Opera House" into the search box and click 🔍.
3. Select your book cover to see a list of related content.

Index

The images in this book are reproduced through the courtesy of: Pandora Pictures, (front cover); Jam Travels, front cover (inset), background (throughout); GagliardiPhotography, front cover (inset); Juli_Step, icon (throughout); heyengel, p. 3; Landscapes & Nature, p. 4; Alexandre.ROSA, pp. 6, 7, 14; Photographic Collection/ Wikipedia, p. 8; -/ SCANPIX DENMARK/ AFP/ Getty Images, p. 9; Russotwin/ Alamy Stock Photo, p. 10; John Carnemolla/ Alamy Stock Photo, pp. 10-11; Len Stone photograph collection/ Wikipedia, p. 12; peangdao, p. 13 (steel); Juhku, p. 13 (concrete); eliosdnepr, p. 13 (glass); NuFa Studio, p. 13; liu yu shan, pp. 14-15; Alexandre ROSA, p. 15 (inset); Nigel, pp. 16-17; Sybille Reuter, p. 18; Jacky Ghossein/ The Sydney Morning Herald/ Fairfax Media/ Getty Images, p. 19; David Carillet, p. 20; leelakajonkij, pp. 20-21; Walter_D, p. 23.